Called to Coddiwomple

Also by Colleen Moyne and published by Ginninderra Press
Time Like Coins

Colleen Moyne

Called to Coddiwomple

Called to Coddiwomple
ISBN 978 1 76109 552 8
Copyright © text Colleen Moyne 2023

First published 2023 by
Ginninderra Press
PO Box 3461 Port Adelaide 5015
www.ginninderrapress.com.au

Contents

Introduction	9
Words on Wings	11
This Journey	12
One Last Thing	16
Rhetorical	17
A Life So Small	19
Books	20
My Grandmother	22
My Father	25
Small But Safe	28
Night Music	29
Take My Hand	31
The Spaces Left	33
I Like Gentle People	35
Not a Snob	36
Coddiwompling	38
Charlie	40
A Greyhound Called Winter	41
My Happy Place	43
Geocache	45
Treasure Seeker	46
Fishing for Tranquillity	47
What Treasures From the Deep	48
Out of Place	50
Mother Nature	51
Cats vs Dogs	53
Dogs in Cars	54
Mary Ann Reserve, Mannum	56
River Walking	57
My Beach	59

Ruts and Ripples	60
Stuff	62
Paring Down	64
If Not Now, Then When?	67
Wish	68
Adventure	69
So Close and Yet so Far	71
Trevor	73
Roots and Tendrils	75
Playing House	76
Possibilities	78
Snail Trails	79
The Nomad Life	80
Epilogue	82

Coddiwomple (KOD-ee-wom-pul) Verb – 'To travel purposefully toward an as-yet-unknown destination.'

Introduction

This is a diary – of sorts – that chronicles my coddiwompling 'coming of age'.

I'm writing this introduction while camped beside a river in the lovely South Australian town of Waikerie. Some parts of the book have been written at picnic tables in public parks, some sitting in a deckchair beside the river, in the forest, in libraries, cafés and some even in shopping centre car parks.

It tells the story – in narrative memoir and verse – of how I came to fulfil a growing desire to explore more of my state of South Australia, and possibly venture into other states as well, in time. I longed for the ability to take off whenever I wanted, and to feel the freedom of coddiwompling around the countryside without the constraints of schedules or time.

I'm now a retired sixty-something-year-old woman and for the past few years, my life has been a simple one that consists of a healthy balance between time for quiet solitude and time to pursue my passion for writing, time with family and a growing brood of grandchildren, involvement with my community and the occasional adventure. The latter is what this story is about. The older I get, the more I feel the pull to explore further and to experience more of life while I still can.

Although the idea of camping or caravanning around our own state has become much more popular since the arrival of the Covid-19 virus, there have always been those who have traded the security of four permanent walls (fondly referred to as 'sticks and bricks') for life on the road – whether temporarily or permanently.

The nomadic life can be as simple as a swag and a backpack

or as luxurious as an eight-metre-long touring van with every modern convenience you can imagine. My plans fell somewhere to the left of centre on the scale. I wanted to be able to travel with only the most basic necessities for myself and my dog.

It has taken quite a few years and a lot of dreaming to get to this point. I am one who changes like the seasons, and what I want today may not be what I want tomorrow.

That restless spirit has always been with me, and so has my need to write.

This story is my way of tying the two together.

Words on Wings

Write your thoughts.
Put pen to paper or hands to keyboard
and write.
Write what bubbles deep inside you.
what churns and roils
wanting to rise to the surface.

Don't write for strangers
or for friends
or for family.
Write for your own heart and soul.
Write to understand, clarify, accept
those bubbling, churning thoughts

and then – should you so desire –
give those words wings and set them free,
send them out into the world,
and chance just may carry them
into the hearts and souls
of strangers, or friends, or family
who need them as much as you do.

This Journey

Why has it taken this long
to learn the true meaning of life?
For all those years,
how did I get it so wrong?
Is it something
that only comes with hindsight
and not when we're young?

Stumbling through the early days,
there were dark tunnels
to be braved,
wrong turns to be righted,
red lights to be waited out
trying to navigate
what it was all about

No maps, no guides, no clues
and even now, sometimes
a stone in my shoe,
a twisted root or two
to trip me up,
a misplaced sign
that leads me, for a time,
in another direction.

But I've learned –
though a little later than I should –
that it's this winding journey
that has been so wonderfully good.
There is no destination
that could surpass – if attained –
the joy of the path trodden
all these years,
the experience gained.
The cliché so often espoused
that 'it's the journey
not the destination that counts',
is the truest thing I know.

There will be an end.
The time will come for me to go,
but destination?
I don't believe so.
Destiny – well, that's another thing.
I was destined
to endure, embrace, explore
and accept all that this life brings.
I was destined to learn and grow
from all these things.

I was raised to believe
that my sole purpose in life,
was to be a dutiful mother and wife.

But now,
with the wisdom
of accumulated years
I can say
That the purpose of life is
to live, love, laugh
and share every day.

Oh…and play –
don't forget to play,
and don't strive
for the destination,
but savour the view
along the way.

The main focus of this story didn't develop when I was a child, or even when I grew up, married and had babies, but there were several events throughout those years that foreshadowed what was to come.

My husband passed away unexpectedly when my children were very young, and the image I had cultivated of the perfect life was shattered. I found myself raising my three beautiful babies alone. They were my whole world, and I was determined to give them the best life I could.

Although finances were limited, I made it work. I had learned from my mother how to live frugally, and I rose to the challenge.

One Last Thing

I've proven I can handle
all that life has thrown my way.
I stood my ground when others
might have turned and walked away.

When times were hard, I managed
to stay strong and make it through.
I weathered all the ups and downs –
now there's one last thing I need to do…

I need to find the courage
to start my life anew
and learn how to live it
without you.

Rhetorical

I was once asked to imagine
that my house was on fire
with my children inside –
and I could only save one.

Which one would it be?
How would I decide?
A rhetorical question, so casually asked,
yet one that defied a response.

Should I choose the first one?
The second or third one?
The clever and creative one?
The brave and resilient one?

The one whose blue ocean eyes
keep the memory of his father alive,
who feels so deeply,
and loves so completely?

But what about the other ones?
The quirky child who shines bright as the sun,
the introspective one
with wisdom beyond her years?

My answer is this –
I would find a way to carry them all
for they are three parts of a whole – three parts of me.
Without the three, the whole would cease to be.

My own childhood was not a happy one. My parents were not happy parents. They were so immersed in the business of day-to-day survival that we children were often left to our own devices. We were quite poor, so there was never money to spend on outings or adventures.

They separated when I was only three years old.

My father went to live with his mother – my grandmother, and I only saw him briefly every two weeks when he came to deliver the 'maintenance' money. He would stay for as long as it took to drink a cup of tea. The interaction between us was tense and detached.

I lived with my mother in a typically suburban home. She battled mental health issues which made her behaviour unpredictable, and because of this, our young lives were difficult and uncertain. We lived in a kind of hermetic cocoon and rarely ventured past the local shops. It was a lonely life. I read books – lots of books – and wrote stories and poetry as a way to understand my world and express my thoughts.

A Life So Small

There was no laughter –
No adventure –
No enriching experiences.

There was school and home
and homework
and television and bedtime

There was silence
and indifference
and walking on eggshells

My life was so small
it fit into the tiny space
between my mother's walls.

Books

There is a special bond
that a lonely child forms
with books –
an unspoken connection
filled with words.

Books can lead a child
from darkness to light,
from strangeness to familiarity,
from boredom
to a world of wonder.

My books led me from the turmoil
and uncertainty of home
into a place of peace
and refuge.

I remember spending small amounts of time at my grandmother's property in the Adelaide Hills whenever my mother was in hospital, which was often.

My grandmother was much like my father – mysterious and detached. My memories of her are of an imposing, no-nonsense woman who would send my sister and me outside to play while she busied herself sewing or bustling about in the kitchen, cooking up all sorts of wonderful meals – much nicer than we had at home.

I was a little afraid of her, but I always looked forward to visiting for the picturesque country location and the freedom of exploring her large property and the nearby forest.

My Grandmother

My grandmother
was just one small thread
in the fabric of my childhood,
yet her passing unraveled me,
disconnected me
from the other me –
the one I was meant to be.

You see, I lived in suburbia –
every day a bore,
a mirror of the one before,
no opportunity to grow and explore.

But holidays at Grandma's
promised fun,
exploding from the car
like pellets from a gun,
we would scatter
into the fields and trees,
barely stopping to say hello,
off we'd go until dusk
chased us home.

My grandmother,
aloof and stern,
hovered on the fringe
of our visits,
accepting our presence,
tolerating our childish games
with an icy silence rarely broken,
words only spoken
as instruction or scolding.

But when her life ended
so did the visits
and the adventure
and the freedom,

and I shrank back to suburbia –
every day a bore,
a mirror of the one before,
no opportunity to grow and explore.

When I was sixteen, my father – quite unexpectedly – invited me on a camping trip with him and my uncle (his older brother.)

I didn't want to go. I hardly knew him – or his brother. I was a young, shy sixteen-year-old girl who had never slept away from home and now I was going to spend ten days alone with them, roughing it in the Flinders Ranges and sleeping outdoors. The experience was so far out of my comfort zone that I was ill-prepared for it, and despite my misgivings, my mother made me go. I still wonder why.

My Father

Who was this man
who hovered in my peripheral view
half-familiar, yet half stranger
to the child he fathered.

He knew my name
and sometimes sent a card
when my birthday was due,

but he never knew
the blossoming teen,
the woman-to-be,
the real, inner me.

When I was married
and my children came,
he barely learned their names.
He couldn't see them
through the wall
he built around himself

and when loss
took us by surprise
and grief
consumed our days,
he busied himself
building the wall higher,
adding more bricks,
shutting us out.

Until I learned not to need him.

And now he is old,
the wall has become his prison.
He sits and stares
through milky windows
of half-awareness…
and has forgotten my name.

The camping trip did little to improve my relationship with my father. It was uncomfortable and awkward, and I missed the familiarity of my own bed, but what I remember the most about the experience was the stunning scenery and dark, star-filled skies of the Flinders Ranges. Suburbia seemed a whole world away.

That was my first experience of the rawness and wild beauty of the mid-north, and it would be quite a few years before I tasted anything like that kind of adventure again.

Small But Safe

Like a child
seeing the ocean
for the very first time,
I gaze wide-eyed
at the expanse of ink-black sky
pierced by a million bright stars
and blanketing the cool earth
with its mass.
Suddenly I feel small…
but safe.

Night Music

When the sun
dissolves into the horizon
and daylight dims,
and the busy-ness of the day subsides,
that's when the night music begins

Against the background hum
of soft breeze
shifting leaves on creaking trees,
comes the rustling sound
of tiny creatures on moss-covered ground
scurrying and foraging
alert to dangers overhead
softly hooting owls and crying nightjars
invisible by day
spend the twilight hours searching for prey
Throaty-voiced frogs and the purring of crickets
join in the singalong…
The music of the night is Mother Nature's song

I was married at twenty-one. My husband was a lovely man who was content to live a simple and predictable domestic life. He passed away after a road accident when my children were young, and although raising them alone was hard and money was an issue, I was determined to give them a different life than I had as a child. I wanted them to have at least some small experience of adventure outside of our daily routine, and at the same time quell that restless spirit that was beginning to tug at me.

I moved to a small country property and encouraged the children to play and explore outdoors. Whenever I could save enough money, I would find a caravan park in a nearby town and take them there for the weekend.

We would sleep in a caravan, explore the local area, feed the ducks and possums and, as a special treat, dinner was hot chips on the beach or in a park, depending on where we were camping. Small pleasures, but ones that have stayed with my children into adulthood and given them a continued love of camping and outdoor adventure.

Take My Hand

My child
this house is your haven,
these walls
keep you safe,

but outside
there is a whole world
waiting
to be explored.

Take my hand
and come with me
out into the world.

Let's take the road
less travelled
and sleep in the forest,
count the stars,

marvel at rolling hills,
at the changing
of the seasons
and, for a time,
roam free.

Now that my children are grown with families of their own, my restless spirit has taken over. I retired from my job and have thoroughly embraced the idea of being able to please myself. Rather than retirement being an ending, for me it has become a wonderful new beginning.

I'm only now blossoming into the person I should have been all along. I've found a unique voice through my writing; I have embraced the satisfying life of a coddiwompler and – as a consequence – I've become an inspiration and role model for my family as they face their own challenges in life.

The Spaces Left

They have grown up,
and the weight is easier to bear.
No more three a.m. feeds
or five a.m. hospital waits.

No more awkward talks
about birds and bees
or peer pressure
or dark temptations.

No more dread
of broken curfews
or relief at the sound of key in door.

They have grown up,
forged their own way,
and the weight is easier to bear.
I now have time to spare,

and the spaces left
are filling with poetry.

I'm an introvert by nature. I find myself easily overwhelmed by too many people, too much noise and too much busy-ness.

I like some people, but not all. It's not easy for me to make friends, and even when I do, I hesitate to open myself up to them.

While I get along with others, there are some personalities that I can only handle for short periods and because of this, I am often misunderstood.

I have no doubt that my unhappy childhood contributed to this aspect of my character, but I've come to embrace that side of myself – flaws and all. I've learned that I'm actually quite likeable.

I Like Gentle People

The ones who listen
as much as they speak,
who consider their words
and use them wisely.

Who don't need to be
the loudest or cleverest
or to force their opinion
in thundering tones.

I like thoughtful people

The ones who read books
and write stories,
whisper in libraries and forests
and sit quietly by rivers.
Who pat stray dogs
and rescue baby birds
and pick up litter
that they didn't drop,

But mostly I like
mysterious people

The ones
who unfold slowly
like the petals of a rose
and keep you wondering
how many more layers to go.

Not a Snob

I know you don't understand
my need to retreat,
to keep my distance
despite your kind approach.
How can I explain
the quickening of pulse,
the stammering of words
without it seeming like reproach?

How do I show
a friendly demeanour,
a willingness to chat
but only to a point and not beyond?
You need to know
that here within my space;
my quiet, private place,
there's no pressure to respond,
so, I function very well
if you don't try to step inside,
don't cross that sacred line
unless invited in.

You see, I'm not a snob
I'm really rather nice
to those who understand
the introvert within.

I enjoy my own company and that of my dog, Winter, a gentle greyhound. I fell in love with her the moment she came into my life, and it soon became part of our routine that whenever I had some free time, I'd bundle her and my lovely old terrier, Charlie into the car, grab a snack and drink, and we would take off – often with no particular destination in mind. I only recently learned the term for it – 'Coddiwompling,' which has become one of my favourite words.

Winter loved the car, loved exploring new places, new sights and scents. Although I didn't know it on a conscious level at the time, the seed was being sown for what was to come…

Coddiwompling

Where to today?
I have no plan.
It's much more fun
to just jump in the car
and follow the sun,
to go where the road goes –
or maybe not.
To meander down
an unexpected path
and find an enchanted spot
where I can pretend
I discovered it first,
and – for a time –
be completely at one
with Mother Earth.

I recently experienced the loss of my sweet old terrier, Charlie. She had been taken from an abusive home thirteen years before, and I had the honour of giving her a new life. She was nervous, highly strung and easily overwhelmed by too much activity, (a bit like me.) I wasn't at all sure that she would adapt well to the life of a coddiwompler.

Sadly, I never got the chance to find out. She passed away peacefully in her sleep at the age of eighteen, just two weeks before our new adventure began.

But I still have Winter. She is a happy, quirky, cuddly character, who is up for anything. She grieved for a time when Charlie passed away, but now she embraces the nomadic life and is great company for me as we travel together.

Charlie

When we met, I knew
that we would be friends.
You were broken
and needed me to mend you.

It took time and patience
but you came to trust
that you were safe with me
and there would always be
food,
shelter,
love.

You are old now
and soon it will be time
to cross the rainbow bridge,
but here in my heart
there will always be
good memories,
gratitude,
love.

A Greyhound Called Winter

I named you Winter
after my favourite season,
because you are
fresh and vibrant
like a crisp winter morning,

not because when we met
you shivered and cowered,
beaten down
by your former life,

but because your new life –
with me –
is a new beginning
like the green, lush richness
of the countryside
we will explore together.

No longer made to sleep
in a concrete cage,
and live only to chase
mechanical rabbits
around a dusty track

Now – with me –
you can be free.

Until recently I owned a mid-sized SUV and spent my free days adventuring to random places with the dogs in tow. I would go coddiwompling – no particular plan, just a tank full of petrol and plenty of charge on my phone.

I would take my time and pull over whenever an opportunity arose to admire the scenery and take a good photo. I'd record points of interest, take side-roads worth exploring and stop in a scenic spot for a picnic lunch. I loved visiting small towns and checking out attractions like galleries, museums and thrift stores. When the budget permitted, I'd stop and spend some money at local shops to support their business.

The only problem was that I could only do day trips – or so I thought.

I had not yet considered other options.

My Happy Place

My heart draws me to go
where green fields
replace cloned suburban houses,
and where Colorbond fences
are not essential decor.
Where stobie poles
and phone towers
give way to swaying grasses
and forests of mottled gum trees.
Where my presence is quietly observed
by curious kangaroos
and the only sounds
are the soothing calls
of contented cows,
and kookaburras
laughing at their own jokes.
Where traffic is sparse
and there is no need
for security patrols
or cameras documenting my day.
Where my heart can rest
and my spirit can breathe
and my soul can mend
and the world – at least my world
– makes sense again.

Although I don't really need an excuse to pack up and go, there are plenty of things to do and see on my travels.

I like to geocache, metal-detect, and even occasionally fish (both the hook-and-worm kind and the magnet kind.)

I also paint and hide rocks on my travels for others to find.

Geocaching is a kind of treasure hunt. I have an app on my phone that alerts me to geocaches in whatever area I'm in. I carry a geocaching kit with small trinkets, spare containers, paper and pencils. Whenever I find a hidden cache, I leave a trinket and, if there is any damage caused by weather or vandalism, I'll repair or replace them.

Geocache

There it is –
barely visible
at the foot of a tree
or under a carefully placed rock.
A tiny treasure, left by those
with a spirit of adventure and discovery.

Always a thrill to find,
I leave a message,
swap one small treasure for another,
re-hide
and leave the scene undisturbed
ready for the next adventurer
to discover.

Treasure Seeker

Out in a field or on the beach,
head bent,
deep in concentration,
I walk a measured grid,
section by section,
listening to the changing tones
of a blue metal detector
as it sways back and forth in my hand
like a wet mop over wooden floors.

Now and then I stop,
alerted by the accelerating beeps
and dig, hoping – this time –
to turn up something special.

But the outcome
is nearly always the same –
bent nails, bits of wire and bottle caps,
each, no doubt, with a story of its own,
a life before rust and decay took hold.

But now their only worth
is in returning their elements
to the earth

Yet my hope never dampens,
my quest for treasure never fades.
I still enjoy the thrill
of following the blue metal detector
as it beeps and sways.

Fishing for Tranquillity

An amateur at best,
I bait the rod
and cast my hope
into the water.

Today – like most days
there will be no fish,
no perch or bream
tugging at the line.

I have no idea
of rigs and lures,
of line weights,
of sinkers and floats,

I fish for the peace
and serenity of water,
for the gentle ripples
and lapping waves.

I never plan
on snaring dinner,
yet somehow always bring home
the best catch of all.

What Treasures From the Deep

I tie a magnet to a string
and toss it into the river,
feel the weight
as it descends into the depths,
and the slackening
as it reaches the bottom.

I drag it slowly,
letting it explore the riverbed
and, like a creeping crustacean,
it seeks out its metal prey.

As it latches on,
I feel resistance
and slowly, ever so slowly
pull it in.
What has it found today?
A lost watch, a fishing rod,
a treasure box?

Not this time (or the last time
or probably the next)
but another rusty bolt
or baked bean can
to add to my collection.

My life of adventure began to accelerate when I worked out how to kit my car out comfortably for overnight camping. With the back seats folded down I could fit a single mattress for myself and a smaller bed for the dogs. I'd carry a cooler with food and water, stackable containers with clothing and essentials, and blackout curtains for privacy when sleeping.

The first night we slept in the car was a trial run at my daughter's house, in the yard, under the carport. The grandchildren thought it was hilarious seeing their granny's car set up for sleeping.

That night was life-changing for me. I was cosy and warm, and it cemented in my mind the possibility of future overnight adventures, of travelling further, for longer, and the chance to experience more of my lovely state of South Australia, and – who knows – maybe the rest of Australia when I'm feeling a bit braver and Covid-19 permits.

Out of Place

Out of place
in humming cities
of windowed towers,

of relentless traffic
and shuffling feet.

Out of place
in tidy suburbs
of red-brick houses

with manicured lawns
and asphalt streets.

I've spun through space
and swirled through time
of restless pursuit,
of round-hole angst
and square-peg dismay

Till I found my place
in this quiet landscape
of whispering trees,

of velvet hills
and fresh-cut hay.

Mother Nature

I hear you calling
and I'm coming to meet you.
Your roads and fields,
your hills and valleys
invite me to pay a visit –
to stay a while
and enjoy your hospitality.

In summer, when you dress
in muted yellows and browns
and tiny creatures
hide in the folds of your gown
waiting for the cool of night.

And in winter, when you wear
green velvet
trimmed with wildflowers
and adorned with diamond raindrops.

I can't wait to meet you,
to see your beauty,
and explore the places
you call home

My greyhound, Winter, is an adventure dog, embracing new places and new experiences. Wherever we go, she draws attention, and the introvert in me has had to accept that – whether I like it or not – people want to interact with us, and their intentions are always good.

While greyhounds are known for their gentle and friendly nature, I'm aware that I am vulnerable as a single older woman, so I try to convey that she is also my protector when the need arises but I'm not fooling anyone. Winter is a definitely a people dog.

Cats vs Dogs

Some people like cats –
What's up with that?
I guess if you like
a hoity-toity housemate
who treats you like a doormat

then get a cat.

If you like to spend your time
playing servant
to a spoilt brat

then I highly recommend a cat.

But if you'd rather be adored,
to be entertained
whenever you're bored,
If you want something to cuddle
and not be ignored

Then get a dog

If you need a companion
on your daily run
or a warm-hearted greeting
when your day's work is done

Then I tell you, my friend,
I'll defend to the end
and highly recommend
man's (and woman's) best friend –
a dog.

Dogs in Cars

Windows down,
face to the breeze,
tongue lolling and jowls quivering,
ears blown back
like the aftershock of an explosion.

I'm fortunate to own a house in one of the most popular tourist towns in South Australia, on the banks of the Murray River, and Winter and I go walking by the water whenever we are there. It soothes the soul and calms the spirit.

There is a quaint beauty in watching paddle steamers lumber by, churning the water as they go, or seeing families picnicking, swinging from ropes tied to trees, or speeding past on jet skis.

During peak tourist times, there is a constant holiday spirit at the local reserves, but off-peak, it settles into a quiet serenity.

Mary Ann Reserve, Mannum

The Murray Princess – stately paddle steamer –
shunts her way lazily along the river.
Her captain's practised spiel
echoes over the loudspeaker
describing the river's history
and relevant landmarks

Excited children
race along the foreshore
avoiding fishing rods
strategically placed
in anticipation of a catch.

They wave to the passing vessel
taking in the magical scene
until, lured back
by the tempting scent of barbecue
they rejoin their families for lunch,
watched over by an audience
of curious pelicans.

River Walking

Walking beside the river,
breathing the damp, earthy air,
watching the water's surface
tremble at the touch
of feathered fishermen
suspended, waiting
to snatch their prey,

I pause,
aware of a subtle shift
in the space above my brow,
a quieting of the chatter
that tends
to roost in the corners
of my brain
scratching, clucking,
making its presence known.

Today that space is different.
Today the river
with its cleansing flow
has silenced the chatter
washing away
the senseless noise,
leaving in its wake
a silent, placid peace.

During tourist season, my hometown fills with families drawn to the river and to local attractions like our monthly markets and car club meets. For some, this is their perfect getaway, but not for me. I prefer the off-peak season when I can have the river all to myself.

So, while lines of traffic are heading into town, I'm heading out, looking for silence and solitude.

When I find a perfect spot, I'm often torn between wanting to tell others about it and wanting to keep it to myself.

My Beach

Freeing my feet
from the confines of sandals,
I step onto the sand
and feel the damp grains ooze
between my toes.

I am alone
on this deserted beach,
a small being in a vast landscape.

Behind me,
green hills hover protectively,
while the vibrant blue ocean
beckons me forward.

The constant lapping of waves
against a weathered sea wall
is the only sound
in this private place.

Others have ventured here before
and will come again,
but today,
these hills, this beach,
and the lapping waves
belong to me.

Ruts and Ripples

Out for a Sunday drive
just my faithful dog and I,
a dirt road off to one side.
piques my curiosity,

I never noticed it before
but now it beckons me to explore,
laying out a welcome mat
of ruts and ripples.

I slow, check the time
and the petrol gauge,
calculate the risk
and, casting previous plans aside,
turn the car.

Who knows what lies ahead?
What treasures might I find?
Perhaps a whole new adventure
of a different kind.

I began to follow the adventures of people on social media who live full-time in a caravan or van. When I saw the lifestyle they had created for themselves, I felt a yearning to experience the same thing. Although I loved my home and the town I live in, I couldn't shake the restlessness that kept calling me away.

I found the idea of living in a small space, paring my needs down to comfortably fit into an area no bigger than my bathroom, quite appealing. If I could camp comfortably in my car with dogs, then a van would be more than ample.

I began to look at my house differently. Who needs all this space? Who needs three bedrooms when you live alone? Who needs a garden when you don't enjoy gardening? The older I get, the simpler my needs have become.

It was time to do something about it.

Stuff

I bought a house, so I needed stuff,
bought chairs and a bed but it wasn't enough.

I filled all the corners with gadgets and things,
I wanted the pleasure that having stuff brings.

I worked at my job every day of the week,
from morning till night, I performed at my peak.

I needed to earn all the money I could
to pay for this stuff that I thought was so good.

But as time was passing my will became lost,
I found that my lifestyle was not worth the cost.

The things I'd acquired to bring me esteem
were no longer part of my future dream.

The time and the money I came to regret.
I was tired of working to pay off my debt.

The joy I had hoped for from all these gains
was now just a burden that held me in chains.

I knew that I needed to turn things around,
to shake off the shackles weighing me down.

I packed up my stuff and I gave it away.
I dreamed of a life of less work and more play.

I soon began chasing another obsession –
A life much simpler and free of possessions

where peace and contentment and freedom suffice.
A life that has value instead of a price.

Paring Down

It begins
with trinkets and things,
a bag of clothing
set aside for donating

Bits and bobs,
once considered meaningful
or necessary
now need no debating

These things,
no longer worth the price
now just clutter blocking the path
to a new and simplified life

Books are the hardest –
Which to keep,
which to re-home?
How many can I take?

Will I come to regret
the decisions I make?

But once my new life begins
it becomes so clear.
My priorities shift
on the things I hold dear.

No longer do I need
that couch or that bed.
I have my sleeping bag
and camp chair instead.

Who needs pictures
adorning the wall
when the view from my van
Is the prettiest of all?

Who needs
artificial light
when I have sun in the day
and the moon and stars at night?

There is no ornament
or trinket I need
when I have wildlife
and flowers and trees.

Sometimes at night
my books go unread
as I recall the day's adventures
and the stories in my head
I have the joy
of warmth in the winter
and shade from the sun.
That is all I need today

and things I thought essential
when my journey began
have been shed like old skin
along the way.

It wasn't easy making the decision, but I needed to quell the nagging thoughts and find out once and for all if what I yearned for was the right thing for me. If I was going to do this, I needed to commit to it fully. I needed to move out of my house and into a van.

Was I crazy?

I broached the subject with my children and was buoyed by their support of the idea. They want me to be happy and to experience more of life going forward.

I began the search for a van. It needed to be the right fit for me – and my dog.

It had to be mechanically reliable and comfortable to live in. I called on the assistance of my son-in-law who, in the past, built out caravans and campervans for a living. I was confident that he would be able to help me.

If Not Now, Then When?

The years quicken their pace,
the days run a constant race
to the inevitable end.
So, if not now, then when?

If not this, then what?

There is so much more
of the world to explore
and who knows
how long we've got?
So, if not this, then what?

And if not here, then where?

Not rooted here
inside these walls,
when the chance for adventure calls
and the road is waiting there.

So, if not here, then where?

Wish

Close your eyes –
Think of the thing
you want the most.
Breathe in…and blow.
Watch the smoke swirl
as it carries your wish
out into the world.

Or raise your eyes
to the evening skies
and wish on the first
star you see.
What will that wish be?

What is it you desire
that a faraway star
can fulfil?

Will you keep wishing
and wishing until
by some miracle
that most coveted thing
comes to pass?
Or will you do your part,
take your own action,
to feed the longing in your heart?

It will never come true
until you make a start.

Adventure

Adventure
is almost in view
around the next corner
or over the next hill

I feel it getting closer.
like waking from a dream
and learning that it's possible
to make it real.

So, I bought a van.

I withdrew most of my meagre superannuation savings and bought a 1996 Toyota HiAce pop-top campervan.

My children named him Trevor – I don't know why – but the name has stuck, and it suits him. He is handsome and immaculate and with low kilometres on the clock. He has a fridge, microwave oven, sink and stove. The seats fold out into a comfortable bed. Trevor is the man – I mean van – I'd dreamt of all this time.

The problem was that Trevor was in New South Wales and the state was in lockdown due to Covid-19.

I had to wait…

So Close and Yet so Far

I can see it, feel it,
almost taste it.
It's right there in front of me –
but only in photographs.

I scrutinise
every detail,
zoom in to inspect
all the angles, nooks and crannies.

I've planned it all –
what will go where,
how it will look.
Everything is in place…

but so is a Covid-19 lockdown.

After months of waiting, I made the decision to have Trevor transported to South Australia by a car-carrier. It was costly, but I didn't want to wait any longer. I was anxious to meet him and start our new life together.

The day he arrived at my house, and I could finally explore all he had to offer, I cried. This little van felt like home.

I knew I had made the right decision.

Trevor

Like finding the perfect match
on a dating site,
I saw you for the first time
and my heart skipped a little.

There you were,
handsome and well-equipped,
not too young and not too old,
steadfast and reliable.

I couldn't wait to meet you,
and when I did –
you were everything
the advertisement promised.

I've found
my happily ever after
and cannot wait
to share life's adventures with you.

I'm fortunate to still own my house with a very affordable mortgage.

One of my children – my oldest daughter – had been searching for a rental home for herself and four children with no luck. It seemed as though we had the perfect solution presented to us. I would rent my house to my daughter until she could find something else, and I would move into the van. That way, I could take my time to decide whether van living was right for me, while still having the security of a 'sticks and bricks' home to return to in the future.

If or when my daughter moves out, I will have the option of selling or renting to someone else. It's a win/win.

Roots and Tendrils

My roots are here
in this beautiful place
but I am growing
beyond the walls,
my branches spreading
to the vast unknown.

With each new adventure
I grow a little more,
my tendrils reaching out
and curling through
the places I visit
absorbing all their goodness.

With each new day
I move further away,
spread new seeds
break new ground.

But this place will always be
where my roots are found.

Playing House

When I was young, I played 'house,'
sat my dolls on chairs
and poured invisible tea
into plastic teacups

I imagined what fun it would be
to grow up
and someday
own a real house

I never imagined what fun it would be
to grow up
and someday trade my house
for a life on the road

I now live full-time in my van, Trevor, with my dog, Winter, and the things most precious to me. I'm amazed at how little attachment I have to the possessions that have been stored away. I carry T-shirts, jeans and a few good shirts that don't need to be ironed (who wants to iron?) There is room for my art and writing supplies, books, board games, camera equipment and Winter's toys, bowls and so on.

I have solar panels so that I can free-camp and have plenty of room to carry my metal detector, fishing rod, folding chair, toolbox and other necessities.

My glovebox is filled with maps and my head is filled with the excitement of what lies ahead each day.

Possibilities

I clear the table
and unfold the map,
spreading it out before me,
smoothing the creases
and marvelling at the vastness of my state.

How shall I do this?
Draw a circle? A spiral?
Close my eyes and stick in a pin?
Go from the inside out
or from the outside in?

The possibilities
are endless and exciting.
I think I'll pack the van
 start the engine and just go
wherever the road
and my heart take me.

Where will that be?
I don't need to know.

Snail Trails

Like the snail
who carries her home on her back,
I make my way, unhurried
through hills and valleys,
down little-travelled tracks

Leaving in my wake
silver trails of memories,
of sights seen, people met –
faces and places
I will never forget

This tiny home
is my comfort zone,
my happy place.
Everything I need
fits in this tiny space

And the things I possess,
that I treasure the most,
that keep my soul fed
Are those faces and places
that will live on forever
inside my head.

The Nomad Life

Sometimes a stranger
is our deepest connection
A cursory greeting,
a fleeting interaction,
perhaps not even a physical attraction
and yet…we can form a bond
with those we've just met

This is the nomad life
on the road to wherever
arriving there whenever
and meeting whoever has chosen
the same destination that day

Whether on holiday
or in a permanent travelling home,
they – like you –
are an ever-rolling stone

and this is where the connection starts –
a chance meeting
of two wandering hearts

Where are you from? Where to next?
Nice dog. What's her name?
They never ask mine; I never ask theirs
but we're connected just the same

Kindred spirits
on separate journeys,
but in the shower block,
around a communal campfire
or over a glass of wine
we meet, connect
and our spirits align

Sharing tales
of the places we've been
and, although we may never meet again,
for the briefest time,
in this special place,
that stranger was a friend.

Epilogue

So, this is my life now.
My home is not a house built of straw or sticks or bricks.
My home is a van – pretty much a large tin can
with a roof and a floor, windows and a door…
and yet, to me, it is so much more.
It holds everything I need or want right now
and keeps me safe at night.
I carry it with me wherever I go,
on whichever path feels right.
My backyard is limitless, boundless,
an ever-changing view
and each morning, when I look outside,
I see something new.
Yesterday I saw ducks on the river
and speedboats dashing by.
Today I see a row of swaying gumtrees
and a sparrow arguing with a curious magpie.
Tomorrow – who knows what delights
my backyard will show?
I guess that depends on when I choose to leave here…
and where I choose to go.

www.ingramcontent.com/pod-product-compliance
Lightning Source LLC
Chambersburg PA
CBHW071027080526
44587CB00015B/2530